The Book of
Scottish Names

THE BOOK OF
SCOTTISH
NAMES

IAIN ZACZEK

ILLUSTRATED BY
JACQUI MAIR

McArthur & Company
Toronto

First published in Canada in 2001
by McArthur & Company Publishers Limited

First published in Great Britain in 2001 by Cima Books
32 Great Sutton Street, London EC1V 0NB

Canadian Cataloguing in Publication Data

Zaczek, Iain
  The book of Scottish names
  ISBN 1-55278-179-8
  1. Names, Personal – Scottish. I. Title
CS2375.S35Z32 2001   929.4'4'09411   C00-932141-1

10 9 8 7 6 5 4 3 2 1

Designed by David Fordham
Illustrations by Jacqui Mair

Typeset by MATS, Southend-on-Sea, Essex
Reproduction by Alliance Graphics, Singapore
Printed in Portugal by Printer Portuguesa

Contents

Introduction 7

Girls' Names 9

Boys' Names 59

Kings & Queens of Scotland 121

Introduction

FEW COUNTRIES CAN BOAST a richer cultural heritage than
Scotland. As a meeting point for many different cultures, it enjoys
a very varied selection of forenames.

The primary influence came from the Scots themselves. They were
a Celtic tribe, who migrated in c.500 AD from northern Ireland to
Argyll, where they founded the kingdom of Dalriada. Their
principal rivals were the Picts, another Celtic people, whose
presence can be traced back to the 3rd century AD. A long war of
attrition ensued, until they were united under the leadership of
Kenneth MacAlpin in 843 – the country's broad base of Gaelic
names derives from this Celtic source.

New names were added by the waves of invaders and settlers who
arrived in later years. Anglian raiders brought Germanic influences
to the Lowlands but more lasting changes came from the Viking
warriors who wielded particular power over the Orkneys, Shetlands
and Hebrides from the end of the 8th century. Their influence
gradually waned in the 13th century, but by this time their cultural
traits were deeply embedded in the Scottish way of life.

By this stage, the most significant influx of newcomers was arriving from the south. The Normans had landed in England in 1066, but it was only in the following century that their impact was felt in Scotland. The driving force behind this development was David I. He grew up at the English Court and, through his marriage to Matilda of Huntingdon, became one of the most powerful barons in the south. When he moved north to claim the Scottish throne, many of his Norman retainers followed him, bringing a whole new raft of names with them.

After the failure of the Jacobite rebellions, there was a long exodus of Scots to other parts of the globe. Many left under tragic circumstances – evicted in the 'clearances' (deportations), which were enforced by the English authorities – ensuring that Scottish names can now be found throughout the English-speaking world.

GIRLS' NAMES

THE early development of girls' names in Scotland is shrouded in darkness. Royal and aristocratic women are well documented in historical records but, for the broader mass of the population, the most useful source material is popular literature. In particular, there is a wealth of information in the ancient ballads, which were transmitted orally for many generations, before being collected in the late 18th and early 19th centuries. Women featured prominently in these, in tales of tragic love (*Fair Helen, Barbara Allan*), sibling treachery (*The Cruel Sister*) and supernatural encounters (*Tam Lin, The Lass of Lochroyan*).

A very varied selection of girls' names can also be found in the writings of Scotland's greatest authors, Burns and Scott. The former's roving eye led him to celebrate the names of many different women in his verses, while the huge vogue for Scott's novels provided the inspiration for numerous children's names, in much the same way that today's parents may be swayed by the popularity of a famous film star or rock musician.

A

ABIGAIL, GAIL

ABIGAIL IS A BIBLICAL NAME, which was borne by one of King David's wives. It was popular in Britain during the Puritan era, and was closely associated with Mrs. Mashum, one of Queen Anne's favorites. In Celtic areas, it became the anglicized form of Gobnait, although the reason for this is unclear. The most celebrated Gobnait was a 5th-century nun, who built a chapel on the site where she witnessed nine white deer. In the 20th century, the abbreviated form, Gail, has become popular in its own right. In Scotland, this may partly be due to the similarity with the word 'Gael'.

Gobnait
(5th century)

ADA

THIS ANCIENT NAME has Germanic roots, stemming from *adal* ('noble'). It was introduced into Scotland by the Normans and was much used during the Middle Ages. The most notable bearer was Ada, the daughter of the Earl of Huntingdon, who was a niece of both Malcolm IV (ruled 1153–65) and William the Lion (ruled 1165–1214). The name underwent a revival in the Victorian era, but is currently out of fashion.

Nessie, the Loch Ness Monster

AGNES, AGGIE

THIS COMES FROM the Greek word for 'pure' (*hagnos*). The name was popularized in the West through St. Agnes, a young Roman martyr who was a victim of Diocletian's persecutions. Her symbol was a white lamb, doubtless because of the similarity to her name (*agnus* is Latin for 'lamb'). In Scotland, Aggie is the most common pet form, but Nesta and Nessie are also used. The latter is better known, of course, as the affectionate nickname of the Loch Ness monster.

Ailsa Craig,
'eagle rock'

AILSA

THIS UNUSUAL NAME (pronounced *AYL-sa*) has its origins in a
geographical feature, the rocky island of Ailsa Craig in the Clyde
estuary. Its root is probably the Old Norse word *alfsigesey*, which stems
from *alf* ('elf') and *sigi* ('victory'), although some believe that the
island's name simply means 'eagle rock'. The decision to use Ailsa as a
personal name was undoubtedly influenced by its similarity to both
Elsa and Ealasaid, the Gaelic form of Elizabeth.

ALISON, ALICE

ALICE WAS INTRODUCED into Britain by the Normans. It originated
as a contraction of *Adalheidis*, a Germanic name meaning 'nobility'.
The pet form, Alison, also came into use in the Middle Ages, proving
especially popular in Scotland. Alison Begbie was a friend of Burns
and may have inspired the verses to *Mary Morrison* (*c.*1781). Alison
Cockburn (*c.*1712–94) was a songwriter, best known for her version
of *The Flowers of the Forest*. In recent years, Allie and Ally have also
become popular, doubtless through the influence of the television
show *Ally McBeal*.

AMY

THIS IS AN ANGLICIZED FORM of the French word for 'beloved'
(*aimée*). The name has been in use since Norman times, but its real
rise to prominence came during the Romantic era. This was due to
the phenomenal success of *Kenilworth* (1821), one of Scott's most
popular novels, which dealt with the mysterious fate of Amy
Robsart, the tragic lover of the Earl of Leicester. More recently,
the name gained added publicity from the exploits of Amy Johnson,
the famous aviatrix.

ANN, ANNE, ANNIE

ORIGINALLY A HEBREW NAME, this is actually a diminutive of
Hannah ('favored by God'). The mother of the Virgin Mary was called
Anne and the name flourished initially in the Byzantine empire, only
finding favor in the West in medieval times. In a Scottish context, it is
most closely associated with a celebrated ballad, *Annie Laurie*. This
was published anonymously in 1838 and later claimed by Alicia Ann
Spottiswood (1810–1900). The song tells of the romance between
Annie and the soldier-poet, William Douglas of Fingland.

ANNABEL, ANNABELLA

ALTHOUGH THIS LOVELY NAME is now commonplace throughout
the English-speaking world, its use was confined to Scotland until
fairly recent times. It stems from the Latin word for 'loveable'
(*amabilis*) and probably developed as an alternative form of Amabel,
which was popular in Anglo-Norman areas. The name has been
current in Scotland since the 12th century, one of the most notable
instances being Annabel Drummond (d.1401), the consort of Robert
III and mother of James I. Annaple is a uniquely Scottish variant,
although it is rarely used today.

Annabel Drummond
(d.1401)

ARABELLA

ALTHOUGH ORIGINATING in Scotland, the name's precise source is
unclear. It may be an alternative to Annabella or a rendering of the
Latin word *orabilis* ('susceptible to prayer'). William the Lion (ruled
1165–1214) is said to have had a granddaughter named Orabilis, but
the name is chiefly associated with the tragic figure of Lady Arabella
Stuart (1575–1615). A cousin of James VI, she had a potential claim
to the throne and was ultimately imprisoned in the Tower of London.

Beathog, a daughter of Somerled

B

BEATHAG

This is a very ancient name (pronounced *BUH-hak*), which stems from the Gaelic word for life (*beatha*). Beathog, a daughter of Somerled, became a nun and founded a church on Uist, while Bethoc, the daughter of King Malcolm II (ruled 1005–34), became the mother of Duncan I (ruled 1034–40), the monarch slain by Macbeth in Shakespeare's play. Another Beathoc was the daughter of Donald III, who ruled twice in the 1090s, and an ancestress of John Comyn, who laid claim to the throne in 1291. In later years, the name was sometimes Latinized as Beatrice. This is still used in Scotland, often under the pet form of Beattie.

BIDDY

This pet form of Bridget used to be extremely popular in Scotland. Although Bridget itself is chiefly linked with an Irish saint, the name was also widely used by the Scots, perhaps because of its associations with an ancient Celtic fire-goddess called Brigid. The many variants include Bride, Bridie, Beesy and Bedelia. The name has lost popularity in recent times, because of the pejorative overtones of the expression, 'an old biddy'.

Brenda, 'flaming sword'

BONNIE

THIS IS A SCOTTISH ADJECTIVE meaning 'pretty' or 'fair', which derives from the French word for 'good' (*bon, bonne*). It is usually applied to women, although Bonnie Prince Charlie is an obvious exception. As a name, it is more common in the US, where its usage may have been influenced by a character in the romantic movie, *Gone with the Wind* (1939), or by the gangster Bonnie Parker (1910–34). More recently, there have been associations with the American singer, Bonnie Raitt, and the speed skater, Bonnie Kathleen Blair.

Bonnie Parker (1910–34)

BRENDA

BRENDA DEVELOPED INITIALLY as a Shetland name. It probably derives from *brandr*, an Old Norse term for a 'flaming sword', although some have seen it as a female form of Brendan. St. Brendan the Navigator (c.486–c.575) is principally associated with Ireland, but he did also visit Iona and the western mainland of Scotland. In the 19th century, the name was further popularized by a character in *The Pirate* (1821), a novel by Sir Walter Scott.

C

CATRIONA

This is a celtic form of Katherine, a name which stems ultimately from a Greek word meaning 'pure'. In Scotland, this variant gained added popularity, following the success of Robert Louis Stevenson's *Catriona*. Published in 1893, this novel was the sequel to *Kidnapped*, which had appeared seven years earlier. It tells of the story of Catriona More, the daughter of a renegade, who embarks upon a perilous romance with David Balfour.

CLARINDA

First used in Spenser's *Faerie Queene* (1596), this name enjoyed a literary vogue in the 18th century. Its Arcadian overtones appealed to Burns, who embarked on a celebrated correspondence with Agnes McLehose (1758–1841) – he using the pseudonym 'Sylvander' and she as 'Clarinda'. He composed ten songs for her, most famously *Ae Fond Kiss*, before they parted forever in 1791.

D

Davina

With its many royal connections, David has long been one of the most favored boys' names in Scotland, and several feminine forms have been employed. The most popular of these is Davina, which has been in use since the 17th century. It probably originated in Scotland, perhaps as a variant of the Celtic name Daimhín ('little deer'). There may also be links with the Irish surname Devine, which is thought to come from a Spanish source (*Da Vinas*). The alternative female forms of David are Davida, Davinia and Davidina.

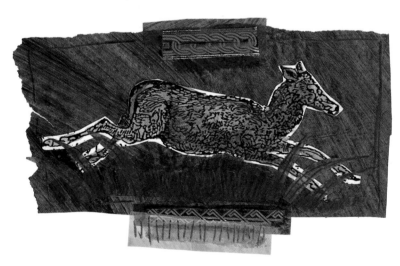

Devorgilla, Devorguilla

Although rarely used today, this name (pronounced *de-VOR-gila*) had patriotic overtones in medieval Scotland. It appears to have developed as an anglicized version of *Diorbhail*, which has been variously interpreted as 'true oath' or 'daughter of the servant'. Either way, it is chiefly associated with Devorguilla of Galloway, who was the mother of John Balliol, king of the Scots (1292–6). She is best remembered as the founder of Balliol College, Oxford, and Sweetheart Abbey in Kirkcudbrightshire. The latter is so-called because, for many years, Devorguilla kept the embalmed heart of her late husband in an ivory casket, before eventually burying it in the abbey.

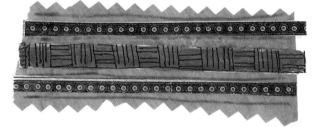

Edina

This is a poetic name for Edinburgh, which derives from *Din Eidin* ('the fortress on the hill'). It was invented by the scholar and political author George Buchanan (1506–82) and was swiftly adopted by successive generations of poets – Burns employed it in his *Address to Edinburgh*. Its use as a personal name is still infrequent, but notable bearers include the actress and fashion designer Edina Ronay and the leading character from the television show *Absolutely Fabulous*.

St. Euphemia (4th century)

EFFIE, EUPHEMIA

MEANING 'FAIR SPEECH', Euphemia (pronounced *you-FEE-mya*)
stems from a 4th-century saint, who was mauled to death by a bear.
The name was widely used in Scotland in the Middle Ages –
Euphemia of Ross was the second wife of Robert II (d.1390), while
Euphame McCalzean was one of the notorious witches of North
Berwick, who were burned at the stake in Edinburgh after
conspiring against James VI. Eventually, the pet form Effie became
more popular. James Boswell (1740–95) had a daughter with this
name, while the critic John Ruskin (1819–1900) entered into a
disastrous marriage with Effie Gray. *Effie Ogilvie* (1886) is the
title of one of Mrs. Oliphant's most distinguished novels.

*Eilidh, a variant
of Helen*

EILIDH, AILEEN

Pronounced *AY-LEE*, this is currently the most popular Gaelic name for Scottish girls. There is some dispute about its origins. Some regard it as one of the many variants of Helen, which means 'radiant one'. Alternatively, it may have developed from Eibhlinn, a Gaelic rendering of Aveline. The Normans were responsible for introducing this Germanic name into the British Isles, where it was rapidly transformed into Evelyn.

EITHNE, EDNA

This name is pronounced *EN-ya* and probably stems from the Gaelic word for a 'nut kernel' (*eithne*), which was traditionally used as a term of praise in ancient Bardic poetry. Alternatively, it may be a female form of Aidan, which derives from *aodhnait* ('little fire'). Several saints bore this name, as did the mother of St. Columba. Eithne is usually anglicized as Edna, although the latter originally came from a Biblical source, referring to the Garden of Eden.

ELIZABETH, LIZZIE, BETTY

A HEBREW NAME meaning 'dedicated to God', this was popularized in the West by St. Elizabeth of Hungary (1207–31). Its Gaelic form is Elisaid or Elasaid. In Scotland, the name had several royal connections, most notably through Elizabeth de Burgh, who was the second wife of Robert the Bruce. Robbie Burns had no fewer than three daughters with this name, two of them illegitimate and a third by Maria Riddell. The pet forms Lizzie and Betty were both extremely popular. Betty Burke was the pseudonym adopted by Bonnie Prince Charlie, when he made his escape to Skye.

ELSPETH

THE MOST POPULAR of the many variants of Elizabeth which are current in Scotland, it can also be found as Elspet, Elspie or Elsie, and its Gaelic form is Elisaid or Elasaid. Scott used the name frequently in his novels, most notably in *Rob Roy* (1817) and *Guy Mannering* (1815). Ultimately, it stems from a Hebrew word meaning 'oath of God'.

ERICA

THIS NAME FIRST ARRIVED in Scotland, as a result of the country's Viking connections. It developed as a feminine form of Eric, which comes from an Old Norse word meaning 'ever brave'. There may also be some link with Oighrig, a Gaelic name which signifies 'new speckled one'. In the 19th century, it gained a new lease of life through a character in Edna Lyall's novel, *We Two* (1884). The fact that *Erica* is the botanical name for heather has given added impetus to its popularity in Scotland.

Esme, Esmé

Meaning 'ESTEEMED' or 'beloved', this name (pronounced *ES-may)* was introduced from France in the 16th century. Initially, it was used as a male name, one of its earliest associations being with Esmé Stuart (1542–83), the High Chamberlain who was created 1st Duke of Lennox. Increasingly though, it was applied to girls, perhaps because of its similarity to Ismay, a female name which had been current since the 13th century.

F

Fenella, Finola

Meaning 'WHITE SHOULDERS', the Gaelic name of Fionnghal (Scotland) or Fionnguala (Ireland) found favor in many Celtic areas. The modern forms of the name are pronounced *fe-NE-la* or *fi-NO-la*. Flora MacDonald was actually christened Fionnghal while, in the 14th century, Torquil MacLeod of Lewis had a daughter named Fynvola. Funnivella and Finella were later forms of the name, while Fenella was popularized by a character in Scott's *Peveril of the Peak* (1823).

Esmé, meaning
'esteemed' or 'beloved'

FIONA

THIS IS A LATINATE FORM of *fionn*, which is Gaelic for 'white' or 'fair'. The name was little used before the 18th century, when it was popularized by a character in the Ossianic poems of James Macpherson. More recently, it has been associated with William Sharp (1855–1905), who wrote a series of visionary, Celtic novels under the pen-name, Fiona MacLeod. Sharp took great pains to conceal his identity, even composing a fake biography for *Who's Who*.

Flora
MacDonald
(1722–90)

FLORA

THE NAME IS OF GREAT ANTIQUITY, originally referring to a Roman goddess of flowers and the spring. It has also gained widespread popularity in Scotland, because of the romantic associations with Flora MacDonald (1722–90). A fervent Jacobite, she helped Bonnie Prince Charlie to escape to the island of Skye by disguising him as her Irish maid. She was imprisoned in the Tower of London for her part in the deed, but was later released and emigrated to Carolina.

FRANCES, FANNY

THIS NAME FIRST BECAME POPULAR in Britain during the Tudor period, proving a particular favorite with members of the nobility. One notable bearer was Frances Stewart, the granddaughter of Lord Blantyre and a mistress of Charles II. She was famed for her beauty and became the model for *Britannia*, as featured on the nation's coinage. Frances Dunlop (1730–1815) was a friend of Burns, and conducted a lengthy correspondence with him.

G

GRIZEL, GRISELDA

Lady Grizel Baillie
(1665–1746)

THOUGH IT IS NOW SOMEWHAT out of fashion, this name has a long history in Scotland. It probably derives from the Old German words for 'grey' (*grisja*) and 'battle' (*hild*). The name rose to prominence through Boccaccio's tale of Patient Griselda, which was popularized in Britain through Chaucer's version of the story. In Scotland, the most common spelling was Grizel. Lady Grizel Baillie (1665–1746) was the daughter of a Covenanter, who courageously organized her father's escape. She found fame as a songwriter and as the founder of a distinguished literary family.

GRUOCH, GRUACH

Gruoch, an ancient Gaelic name

ALTHOUGH RARELY ENCOUNTERED nowadays, Gruoch, pronounced *GROO-ak*, is an ancient Gaelic name, dating back to the early days of Scottish history. Its oldest form was Gróa, which has been linked with a 10th-century countess of Caithness. Gruoch's decline in popularity may be due to the fact that it was Lady Macbeth's name. She may not have been as evil as Shakespeare painted her, though there are hints that she conspired to seize the crown for Lulach, her son by a former marriage.

Heather, one of Scotland's national symbols

H

HEATHER

THIS DERIVES FROM THE MIDDLE ENGLISH word *hathir*. Its spelling was altered in the 18th century, because of the presumed links with 'heath'. Heather's popularity as a personal name dates from the late 19th century, when the 'language of flowers' was much in vogue. In this context, purple heather signifies admiration or beauty in solitude, whilst white heather is believed to offer protection from danger. In a more general sense, heather is regarded as one of Scotland's national symbols.

Helen, Nellie

This is a greek name meaning 'the radiant one', which ultimately stems from *helios* ('the sun'). It became popular in the West through association with St. Helena (c.255–330), the mother of Constantine the Great. Many legends were attached to her name, most notably that she discovered the True Cross (the cross on which Christ was crucified). In medieval Britain, there was also a tradition that she came from native stock. Geoffrey of Monmouth claimed that she was the daughter of Coel (the *Old King Cole* of the nursery rhyme). These beliefs undoubtedly helped to popularize the name in the British Isles.

In Scotland, the name is most closely associated with *Fair Helen of Kirkconnell*, one of the best-known *Border Ballads*. In this tragic tale, the eponymous Helen fell in love with Adam Fleming of Kirkpatrick. She also had a rival suitor, however, who enjoyed her family's approval. As a result, the young lovers used to meet in secret in the local churchyard. At one of the these clandestine meetings, they were surprised by the rival, who shot and killed the maiden.

Hilda

This is a germanic name meaning 'battle maiden'. It gained currency in Scotland through two main avenues – Scottish links with Scandinavia and the cult of St. Hilda (614–80). The latter was mainly active in Northumbria and is best remembered as the founder of the Abbey of Whitby. Although not a Scot, she was venerated in the Borders, especially as she championed the Celtic cause at the Synod of Whitby (664). In Scott's *Ivanhoe* (1819), there is a character named Hilda of Middleham.

St Hilda (614-80)

Ing's golden boar

1

INGEBORG, INGRID, INGA

THE SCOTS BORROWED several Scandinavian names which derived from an ancient fertility god called Ing. According to legend, he rode upon a golden boar with huge tusks, which ploughed up the earth so that farmers could plant their seeds. Ingeborg or Ingibjorg was the most widely used of these imported names, largely because of the fame of Ingeborg of Orkney. She was the first wife of Malcolm III (ruled 1058–93) and the mother of Duncan II, who was murdered after ruling Scotland for just six months in 1094.

IONA, IONE

THIS CHARMING NAME, pronounced *eye-OWE-na*, comes from the small island in the Hebrides which played such an important part in Scotland's early history. St. Columba began his mission on Iona, founding a monastery there in 563. It was also, for a time, the burial place of Scottish kings. Despite the obvious similarities, Ione stems from a very different source. It refers to Ionian Greece and its use dates from the early 19th century, when the Greek War of Independence inspired pro-Hellenic sentiments throughout Europe.

Isabel, Isobel, Ishbel

Isabel emerged as a Spanish variant of Elizabeth. Its Gaelic form is Iseabail and, in Scotland, its most common, anglicized spelling is Isobel. The name has many royal links. Isabella of Mar was the first wife of Robert the Bruce, while Isobel of Fife set the crown upon his head. In other fields, Isobel Baillie (1895–1983) found fame as an opera singer, while Ishbel Gordon, Lady Aberdeen (1857–1939) was a noted philanthropist.

Isla

Pronounced *EYE-LA*, the use of this name was probably inspired by the Hebridean island of Islay, although there is also a River Isla in Perthshire. In recent years, it has been popularized by the singer and television presenter, Isla St. Clair, and by the actress Isla Blair. Islay is sometimes found as a boy's name, but this is rare.

River Isla

J

JACOBINA, JACOBA

THE ORIGINS OF THIS UNUSUAL NAME lie in *Jacobus*, the Latinized form of 'James'. It dates back to the Middle Ages – in 1388, for example, Sir John Hamilton of Cadzow married a girl called Jacoba – but it reached the peak of its popularity at the time of the Jacobite rebellions (1715 and 1745). In the aftermath of these disasters, many Scottish parents chose to christen their children with patriotic names. Jamesina was another alternative.

The white cockade, symbol of the Jacobites

Janet,
from the tale
of Tam Lin

JANET

Oᴿɪɢɪɴᴀʟʟʏ ᴀ ᴅɪᴍɪɴᴜᴛɪᴠᴇ ᴏғ ᴊᴀɴᴇ, this has long been used as an independent name. Its Gaelic equivalent is Seonaid, and both Jenny and Jinty are recognized pet forms. In the past, Jonet and Janetta were also employed, but these are now virtually obsolete. There are several characters called Janet in Scott's novels, most notably in *The Fortunes of Nigel* (1822), and the name crops up frequently in Scottish folklore. In the tale of *Tam Lin*, for example, a young maid called Janet falls in love with an elfin knight (Tam Lin) and becomes pregnant by him. She passes this news to her sweetheart, imploring him to come away with her, but Tam is held under an enchantment by the Queen of the Fairies. In order to rescue him, Janet must steal him away from a fairy procession at Halloween. Bravely, she follows Tam's instructions and, even though the fairies try to hold onto their knight by transforming him into a snake, an eel, and a red-hot iron, Janet clings fast to her lover and wins him in the end.

JEAN

THIS HAS LONG BEEN one of the most popular names in Scotland. It evolved out of the Old French name *Jehane*, which was introduced into Britain by the Normans. In aristocratic circles, Jean Abernethy was the mistress of the Duke of Albany, while James V (d.1542) had an illegitimate daughter called Jean with Elizabeth Bethune.

More famously, Jean Armour (1767–1834) was the loyal wife of Robbie Burns. She bore him nine children and remained devoted to him, even though at one stage he contemplated running off to Jamaica in order to escape his responsibilities. Burns wrote 14 songs for her, the most celebrated of these being *Of a' the airts the wind can blaw*. Jean Adam (1710–65) was herself a poet, best remembered now for *There's nae luck aboot the hoose*, while Jeannie Robertson (1908–75) was a noted balladeer.

JENNY

VARIOUSLY EMPLOYED as a pet form of Janet, Jennifer or Jean, this name has been popular in Scotland since the Middle Ages. During the furore over the introduction of the *Book of Common Prayer* (1637), Jenny Geddes is said to have hurled a stool at the Bishop of Edinburgh. Burns had a mistress called Jenny Clow, a 20-year-old serving girl from Fife. She bore him a son in 1788, but died just three years later.

JESSICA

ORIGINALLY, THIS comes from the Hebrew name Iscah or Jesca, which means 'watched over by God'. Shakespeare appears to have been inspired by this when he created the character of Jessica, Shylock's daughter, in *The Merchant of Venice* (1596). The name has proved very popular in Scotland, largely because of its similarity to Jessie. Its profile has also been raised by the success of the American actress, Jessica Lange. In terms of usage, it is currently one of the top 50 Scottish names.

JESSIE

THIS PROBABLY DEVELOPED as a pet form of Janet, although similar claims have also been made for Jean and Jessica. Its Gaelic form is Teasag. It has long been used as an independent name, largely because of the phenomenal popularity of Robert Tannahill's song, *Jessie, the Flower o' Dunblane* (1807). Tannahill (1774–1811) was a Paisley weaver, who achieved brief success with his lyrics, before drowning himself after a publisher rejected his work. The 'Jessie' in the song was a local girl, Janet Tennant (1770–1833).

JOAN

ORIGINALLY A CONTRACTION of the Old French *Johanne*, this name has been popular in Scotland since Norman times. Alexander II (ruled 1214–49) and David II (ruled 1329–71) both had queens named Joan, the latter sharing her husband's captivity in England. Similarly, Joan Beaufort married both James I (d.1437) and Sir James Stewart, who is better known as the 'Black Knight of Lorne'.

K

KELLY

ALTHOUGH USUALLY ASSOCIATED with Ireland, Kelly was also a popular name in Scotland. It probably originated from *celleach* ('a hermit'), but its main development was as a territorial surname. In Scotland, for example, the principal Kelly estates were at Arbroath in Angus, though there were also Kellie lands at Pittenweem in Fife. Under the influence of American and Canadian usage, Kelly has become an increasingly popular choice as a girl's first name.

KIRSTY, KIRSTIE

THIS POPULAR NAME is a pet form of Christina, which in turn is a contraction of Christiana ('follower of Christ'). The spelling probably derives from Kirsten, a Scandinavian variant of the same name. Its use in Scotland dates back to the 19th century, when Kirstie Elliott was a character in Robert Louis Stevenson's *Weir of Hermiston* (1896). In recent years, it has become extremely fashionable, popularized by such figures as the actress, Kirstie Alley, and the singer-songwriter, Kirsty MacColl.

KYLIE, KYLA

THERE IS CONSIDERABLE DISAGREEMENT about the source of this name. Some believe that it comes from an Aborigine word for a boomerang (*garli*). It is more probable, however, that it developed as variant of Kelly or Kayleigh. There have also been suggestions that it is a feminine form of Kyle, although the normal version of this is Kyla. In any event, the current popularity of the name is undoubtedly due to the phenomenal success of the Australian actress and singer, Kylie Minogue.

Kylie Minogue

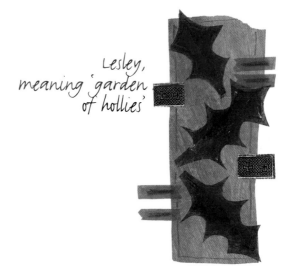

Lesley, meaning 'garden of hollies'

L

LESLEY

THIS IS THE TRADITIONAL FEMALE SPELLING of Leslie, which probably originated as a place name meaning 'garden of hollies'. The first recorded bearer of the name was Lesley Baillie (d.1843), who hailed from Mayfield in Ayrshire. She became the object of Robbie Burns' affections, after their meeting in 1792, and inspired some notable verses. These include the songs, *O saw ye bonnie Lesley* (1792) and *Blythe hae I been on yon hill* (1793). Their acquaintance was very brief, however, and she later married Robert Cumming of Logie.

LILIAS, LILLIAS

THIS IS PROBABLY A FLOWER NAME, deriving from the Latin word for 'lily' (*lilium*), although some prefer to see it as a pet form of Elizabeth. In most English-speaking countries, the preferred spelling is Lillian, but this variant has always been popular in Scotland. One of the best-known bearers of the name was Lilias Drummond, the so-called Green Lady, who is said to haunt Fyvie Castle. According to legend, she inscribed her name in the bedchamber, when her husband remarried shortly after her death.

LORNA

THIS NAME WAS ACTUALLY INVENTED BY an English writer, R.D. Blackmore (1825–1900), who used it for the heroine of his most famous work, *Lorna Doone* (1869). In the novel, she is eventually identified as an aristocrat, Lady Dugal. The action of the book is set in Devon, but Blackmore appears to have borrowed the name from Lorne in Argyll, the ancestral home of the MacDougalls. As a result, the name has become increasingly popular in Scotland.

*Lorna Doone (1869)
by R.D. Blackmore*

LINDSAY, LINDSEY

THIS IS THOUGHT TO BE a territorial name. It may stem from the Norman lands of De Limesay near Rouen, or else from a Romano-British site near Lincoln (a combination of the Latin word *Lindum* and the Old English suffix *-ey*). Either way, it became established in Scotland as the family name of the Earls of Crawford. Sir Walter de Lindeseya was a follower of David I (ruled 1124–53) and one of his descendants was Sir David Lindsay of the Mount – the poet who challenged James V to a 'flyting' (a duel of poetic insults). The name was originally confined solely to boys, but it is now applied principally to girls.

M

Malvina

Malvina (pronounced MAL-VEE-NA) appears to be an invention of the Scottish poet, James Macpherson (1736–96). In his epic cycle about Ossian, a legendary Celtic hero, Malvina was the wife of a warrior named Oscar. Following his death in battle, she was so stricken with grief that her tears turned the heather white. Macpherson may have based the name on *malamhina*, a Gaelic word for 'smooth brow', though the name was also treated as a feminine form of Melvin. There is no apparent connection with *Las Malvinas*, the Argentine name for the Falklands.

Malvina, whose tears turned the heather white

MARGARET

St. Margaret
(c.1045–93)

THIS ANCIENT NAME stems from a Greek word for 'pearl' (*margaron*), which the Normans amended to Marguerite. Its popularity in Scotland dates back to the 11th century, when St. Margaret (c.1045–93) reigned as Scotland's queen. The sister of Edgar the Atheling (the Saxon heir to the English throne), she married Malcolm III in 1069 and soon became renowned for her charitable deeds. She was canonized in 1250.

The name has many other royal associations. The tragic 'Maid of Norway' (1283–90) was also called Margaret. This Norwegian princess was the granddaughter of Alexander III and inherited the Scottish throne upon his death (1286). In spite of her tender years, plans were formulated for a diplomatic marriage, but Margaret died in the Orkneys, before the match could take place. Subsequent bearers of the name have included 'False' Margaret, an impostor who claimed the throne in 1300, and the present Princess Margaret, who was born in Glamis Castle.

*Marjorie, from
the herb marjoram*

MARGERY, MARJORIE

MARGERY WAS A MEDIEVAL VARIANT of Margaret. It has become
synonymous with Marjorie, even though this may have derived from
the herb, marjoram. The Gaelic form, Marsali, is also popular. The
name has close connections with Scottish royalty. Both William the
Lion and Robert the Bruce had daughters called Margery, the latter
becoming the mother of Robert II. More recently, Marjory Fleming
(1803–11) gained fame as a child author, before her untimely death
from meningitis.

MARIA

THIS LATIN FORM OF MARY, which is chiefly used in Mediterranean
areas, has also enjoyed periodic popularity in Britain. Its most
significant revivals occurred in the 18th and 20th century. In
Scotland, the name is most closely associated with Maria Riddell
(1772–1808), a noted poet and a friend of Burns. In recent times, its
profile has also been raised by the heroine of *West Side Story* (1957)
and by the success of the singer, Mariah Carey.

Mariota, Marion

In medieval times, Mariota (pronounced *mar-EE-ota*) was a popular name in Scotland, but it gradually slipped out of use. Its origins are uncertain, though it appears to have developed as a variant of Margaret. The name of Mariota Stewart has entered Scottish folklore, for it is said that she haunted Garth Castle, after being murdered by her husband. In the later Middle Ages, Mariota was superseded by Marion, which has remained a consistent favorite north of the border.

Mary

This is an anglicized form of the Hebrew name Miriam, which may mean 'star of the sea'. It was widely used in medieval Europe, owing to the popular cult of the Virgin Mary. The name has gained particular resonance in Scotland, however, through its tragic associations with Mary Queen of Scots (1542–87). She acceded to the Scottish throne when she was just six days old and, through her marriage to François II, was briefly queen of France. Fatally, though, she also had a claim to the English throne and this led Elizabeth I to imprison her for many years, before finally giving the order for her execution. Four of the queen's ladies-in-waiting shared her name and, as 'the Four Maries', they later became the subject of a famous ballad.

In literary circles, the name is also associated with 'Highland Mary', the shadowy muse who inspired some of Burns' finest poetry. The daughter of a seaman named Archibald Campbell, she and Burns are said to have exchanged Bibles, as a token of their intention to marry, but Mary was carried off by typhus before they could cement their union.

Maureen

This is an anglicized form of Máirín, which means 'little Mary'. It has a long pedigree in Scotland. St. Mungo (d.612), who evangelized the Strathclyde region, had a sister called Muirenn. In the following century Hungus, a king of the Picts, had a daughter named Mouren. In recent times, Maureen McIlwraith has forged a reputation with her atmospheric Celtic novels, most notably in *The Haunted Mountain* (1972) and *The Mermaid Summer* (1988).

Meg

This pet form of Margaret has always been popular in Scotland, and is increasingly being used as an independent name. Meg Hyslop ran the Globe Tavern in Dumfries and was a friend of Burns, while Meg Merilees was a gypsy queen in Scott's *Guy Mannering* (1815). Scott was also instrumental in securing the return of *Mons Meg* (a spectacular cannon) to Edinburgh, after the English had removed it to the Tower of London. Perhaps the most famous bearer of the name, however, was 'Hairy Meg', an infamous brownie (elf), who used to steal babies by stretching her hairy paw down chimneys.

Moira

This is a popular variant of Mary, the Scottish equivalent of the Irish name Maura. It is very well represented in the world of art and entertainment. The Scottish ballet dancer, Moira Shearer, won international acclaim for her starring role in *The Red Shoes* (1948). The South African Moira Lister also found fame as an actress, while Moira Anderson has been a stalwart of the Scottish music scene.

MORAG

Morag, the great and high sun

ONE OF THE MOST POPULAR NAMES in medieval Ireland was Mór, which means 'great' or 'tall'. By extension, it can also be interpreted as a reference to the sun ('the great one'). In Scotland it was more commonly found in a pet form, such as Moreen or Morag – the latter combining Mór with the suffix -ag, which means 'young'. Morag (pronounced *MOE-rag*) used to be confined to Scotland, but the name is now known throughout the English-speaking world. It is sometimes employed as the Gaelic equivalent of Sarah, though the reasons for this are unclear.

MURIEL

THIS IS AN ANCIENT CELTIC NAME, which derives from *Muirgheal* ('sea-bright'). It was first recorded in Brittany in the 11th century, and was brought to Scotland by Norman adventurers. Early documented references include Muriel de Landeles, who was resident in Kelso in 1174, while Muriel de Polloc made grants to the Abbey of Kinloss in 1225. In the 16th century, Muriel Calder was heiress to the Thanedom of Cawdor. In recent years, the name has been popularized by the Edinburgh-born author Muriel Spark, who is most famous for *The Prime of Miss Jean Brodie* (1961). There are several variants of the name, most notably Muriella and Muireall.

 N

NAN, NANCY

THIS ORIGINATED AS A PET FORM of Ann and its Gaelic form is Nandag. Burns also used it as a nickname for Agnes. He wrote *My Nanie O*, along with a number of other songs, for a farmer's daughter called Agnes Fleming. More famously, he immortalized Poosie Nansie's Tavern in Mauchline, using it as a setting for his verse cantata, *The Jolly Beggars* (c.1785). The inn took its name from the landlady, Agnes Gibson (a *poosie* being a slang term for a woman).

Muirgheal, 'sea-bright'

Nora, Norah

Although it is now used as an independent name, Norah originated as a diminutive of other words. It is usually linked with Honora or Honoria, a saint's name which was popular with the Anglo-Normans. Alternatively, it may have stemmed from one of the variants of Eleanor or Leonora. In the Highlands, it was also used as a female form of Norman, referring to the invaders from the south.

Oona, from 'uan', meaning lamb

O

Oona, Oonagh, Una

Mainly used in Scotland and Ireland, this name (pronounced *oo-na*) has disputed origins. The likeliest source is *uan*, an Irish word for 'lamb'. Or, like Unity, it may stem from the Latin for 'one' (*unus*). Spenser probably had this in mind when he created Una in the *Faerie Queene* (1596). In Celtic lore, Una was the queen of the western fairies. More recently, the name has been associated with Oonagh Chaplin, the wife of the comic actor.

P

PEGGY

A PET FORM OF Margaret, this name has proved extremely popular in Scotland and in neighbouring countries. The Gaelic forms are Peigi or Peigín. Burns had several friends with this name. Peggy Thomson was a childhood sweetheart, and he later wrote a song for *Bonny Peggy Alison*. Just south of the border, Peg o' Nell and Peg Powler were regarded as malevolent water spirits.

Peggy Thomson,
childhood sweetheart
of Robbie Burns

R

REBECCA, BECKY

THIS ANCIENT NAME stems from Hebrew or Aramaic, and may originally have meant 'a heifer'. In the Old Testament, Rebekah was the wife of Isaac. The name was introduced into the Highlands at an early stage, where it was used as an anglicized form of Beathag. Rebekah Carmichael was an 18th-century poet. Burns subscribed to a book of her verse, which was published in 1790. Rebecca is currently the second most popular name in Scotland.

Rebekah,
wife of Isaac

Rona, meaning 'seal'

RONA, RHONA

A CERTAIN AMOUNT OF MYSTERY surrounds this charming name. Its origins may lie in one of several Scottish islands called Rona (from *hraun-ey*, Old Norse for 'rough isle'). Alternatively, it may be a female form of Ronan, the saint's name which stemmed from a Gaelic word for 'seal' (*ron*). Equally, it may have developed out of Ragnhild, a name which was very popular amongst the many Scandinavian settlers.

ROWENA

THIS GAINED POPULARITY in Scotland following the success of Sir Walter Scott's novel *Ivanhoe* (1819), which featured a heroine called Rowena of Hargottstanstede. Scott may simply have chosen the name as a variant of Rowan, although it has a long pedigree in its own right. It probably stems from the Welsh name, *Rhonwen* ('fair hair') and was also mentioned in the 12th-century chronicles of Geoffrey of Monmouth.

S

SANDRA, ALEXANDRA

THE USE OF THIS NAME dates back to the Middle Ages, when three
kings called Alexander played a formative role in Scotland's early
history. This royal connection was revived in 1863, when Princess
Alexandra of Denmark married the Prince of Wales (the future
Edward VII). More popular now, however, is the shortened form of the
name, which comes from the Italian Alessandra. It appears to have
been introduced by George Meredith's novel, *Sandra Belloni* (1864).
Saundra is a rare but exclusively Scottish variant.

SHEENA

THIS IS A PHONETIC RENDERING of Sine, a Gaelic name which is
popular in both Scotland and Ireland. Its nearest English equivalents
are Jane or Jean, both of which mean 'God is gracious'. There is also a
Gaelic pet form, Sineag. In modern times , the name has been given a
higher profile by Sheena, a female equivalent of Tarzan. Her
adventures were the basis for a number of comic books (from 1938)
and a television series. Sheena has become increasingly popular in
recent years, following the success of the singer, Sheena Easton.

SHELAGH

THIS NAME (PRONOUNCED *SHE-la*) stems from Cecilia, a name which
was popularized in Western Europe by the 2nd-century saint, revered as
the patroness of music and musicians. In medieval art, her traditional
attribute was an organ. In Scotland, the name was often rendered as
Cicely or Cissie, while in Gaelic-speaking areas it was translated as Síle.
This in turn was anglicized as Sheila. The *-agh* suffix gives the name a
more Celtic flavour, but has no historical or etymological basis.

SHONA

NOW BECOMING INCREASINGLY popular, Shona (pronounced *SHOW-na*)
is an anglicized form of two Gaelic names, Seónaid (pronounced *shone-
AID*) and Seonag (pronounced *SHONE-ag*). Seónaid is the equivalent of
Janet, a name which has been popular in Scotland since Norman times.
It has undergone a recent revival, largely because of the vogue for its
Irish counterpart, Sinead. Seonag is the Gaelic version of Joan.

Sibyl, Sybil, Sibylla

According to classical legend, the sibyls were female seers, entrusted with the secrets of the gods. The medieval Church regarded them as pagan counterparts of the Old Testament prophets, because they had foreseen the coming of Christ. As a result, Sibyl – or, more commonly, Sibylla – became an acceptable name in Christian countries. It was introduced into Britain by the Normans. In Scotland, the most notable bearer was Sibylla, the consort of Alexander I (ruled 1107–24). Nowadays, Cybil or Cybill is the usual spelling.

Sibyl, entrusted with the secrets of the gods

Skye

This is one of several Scottish names, which relate to an island. For many people, it conjures up romantic associations with the escape of Bonnie Prince Charlie, as commemorated in the *Skye Boat Song*. As a result, the name has always exerted a particularly strong appeal for expatriate Scots, and it is most widely used in the US and Canada. The name of the island stems from a Gaelic word for 'knife' (*sgian*), perhaps referring to the deep cuts in Skye's coastline.

T

THORA

THIS IS ONE OF THE MANY Scandinavian names, which Viking raiders brought to Scotland. It relates to Thor, the Norse god of thunder. The name was most common in the Orkneys, where there were close associations with St. Magnus (d.1116). According to the *Orkneyinga Saga*, his mother was a woman named Thora, who married Erlend Thorfinnsson, the Earl of Orkney. After Magnus's death, Thora arranged for his burial at Christ Church on Birsay, where miracles soon began to occur.

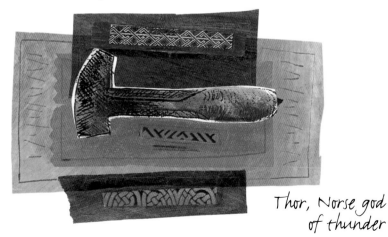

Thor, Norse god of thunder

W

WENDY

THE NAME OF WENDY was invented by the Scottish author, J.M. Barrie (1860–1937), and was first used for one of the central characters in *Peter Pan* (1904). He is said to have taken it from the nickname 'Friendy-Wendy', which was given to him by the daughter of the poet, W.E. Henley (1849–1903). The continuing popularity of *Peter Pan* has helped the name to retain its enduring appeal.

WILLIAMINA, BILLIE

GIVEN THE PATRIOTIC APPEAL of William Wallace, female versions of his forename have always been popular. Williamina, Wilhelmina and Willielma used to be the chief variants, although the modern pet form, Billie, is now much more common. Wilhelmina Alexander (1756–1843) was a friend of Robbie Burns, providing the inspiration for his song, *The Bonny Lass of Ballochmyle*. Similarly, Williamina Belsches was a sweetheart of Sir Walter Scott.

Boys' Names

Ancestry has always played a large part in the Scottish psyche, helping to preserve a significant body of traditional names. In typical Celtic fashion, early Scottish surnames were often made up of a prefix meaning 'son of' (*mac*), followed by the parental forename. This is comparable with the Irish *ua* (later *o'*) and the Welsh *ap*. In Scotland, this custom was reinforced by the clan system, which honored the memory of its founder. Since this ancestor was either an important historical leader or a legendary figure, the founder's name usually conjured up romantic associations with the nation's past. Expatriate Scots often adopted their clan name as a middle name as a means of maintaining their cultural roots. In time, these have frequently come to be used as forenames, particularly in the US.

Unlike some other Celtic areas, the direct use of saints' names was fairly uncommon, largely because the practice was deemed presumptuous. Instead, Scots tended to attach the names to a respectful prefix, such as *maol* or *gille* ('servant of'), as demonstrated by 'Malcolm' and 'Gilchrist'.

A

Adam

THIS IS A HEBREW NAME, deriving from *adama* ('earth'). Its Biblical
associations have ensured its continuing popularity in many Christian
countries, while Scotland has produced two unusual variants. Edom,
the broad Scots equivalent of the name, is celebrated in one of the
best-known Border Ballads, *Edom o' Gordon*. Similarly, the pet form
is linked with St. Adamnan ('little Adam', c.628–704), the biographer
of St. Columba. Famous Scottish bearers of the name have included
Adam of Dryburgh (c.1140–1212), an influential churchman, and
Adam Smith (1723–90), the pioneering economist.

Aidan

ORIGINALLY AN IRISH NAME, Aidan (pronounced *AYD-en*) has
always been widely used in Scotland. It comes from *aodh*, which means
'fire'. The most famous bearer of the name was St. Aidan (d.651), who
was a monk at Iona, before travelling as a missionary to Northumbria,
where he founded the monastery of Lindisfarne. In art, his traditional
attribute is a stag. Prior to this, there was a king of Dalriada called
Aedán (574–606), who was consecrated by St. Columba himself.

St Aidan (d. 651)

Young Aikin

AIKEN, AIKIN

ALTHOUGH RARELY USED TODAY, this name (pronounced *AY-kin*)
will be familiar to many Scots from the nursery rhyme, *Aiken Drum*.
This describes a strange character, who wears edible clothes (a hat of
cream cheese, a coat of roast beef, and so forth). The pedlar-poet
William Nicholson used the same name to describe the Brownie of
Blednoch, who terrified the children of Galloway. In the Border
Ballads, *Young Aikin* told the tale of a forester, who abducted the
king's daughter and kept her hidden for seven years in a treetop-bower.

AINSLEY

PRONOUNCED *AYNS-LI*, this name, originally a surname, is
now increasingly finding favor as a forename. The family had
Norman roots, borrowing their name from their English estates –
perhaps at Annesley in Nottinghamshire. By the early 13th century,
they were established in Scotland. William de Anslee is recorded
as a canon of Glasgow in c.1220. The forename is currently used for
both boys and girls.

ALEXANDER, ALASDAIR, ALISTAIR

IN ITS MANY FORMS, this has become one of the most popular names in Scotland. Alexander came from a Greek name, meaning 'defender'. In antiquity, it was made famous by Alexander the Great (356–323 BC). His exploits were recounted in a host of medieval romances, and it was doubtless one of these which inspired St. Margaret to name a child after him. In the event, there were three Scottish kings called Alexander, and these helped the name to become established. In later years, it became associated with Alexander Selkirk (1676–1721), the Scottish sailor whose travels inspired *Robinson Crusoe* (1719), and Alexander Graham Bell (1847–1922), the inventor of the telephone.

Alexander
Selkirk (1676–1721)

Alexander has remained in use, but the Gaelic forms – Alasdair or Alistair – have matched it for popularity. Of the many abbreviated versions Sandy is probably the most widely used, but Alec, Alick and Sawney are further variants. The former was publicized by the golfer, Sandy Lyle, while Sawney Bean was a notorious 14th-century robber.

ALPIN

ALTHOUGH NOW FAIRLY SCARCE, Alpin is still occasionally used today, on account of its patriotic overtones. The name is thought to be Pictish and its meaning is unknown. Several Pictish kings bore the name, but the most famous Alpin was a Scot. He fathered Kenneth MacAlpin, the man who managed to unite the Scots and Picts under a single crown, thereby becoming the first King of Scotland in 843. In recent years, the most notable bearer of the name has been the writer, Alasdair Alpin MacGregor.

ANDREW

THIS IS AN ANGLICIZED FORM of the Greek name Andreas, which stems from andr ('man' or 'warrior'). The name has been a perennial favorite in Scotland, ever since St. Andrew was adopted as the nation's patron saint.

St. Andrew was a Galilean fisherman, one of the twelve apostles. His cult was widespread in Europe, not so much because of the account in the New Testament, but rather through the apocryphal *Acts of Andrew* (3rd century), which were retold in *The Golden Legend* (13th century). These helped the saint to become so popular, that he was selected as the patron saint of both Russia and Greece, as well as Scotland.

The links with Scotland stem from a myth that the saint's bones were transferred there by a monk called Regulus (or Rule) of Patras. An angel appeared to Regulus and instructed him to carry the relics 'towards the ends of the earth'. When the monk reached the site of modern-day

St. Andrews – the home of the famous golf course – the angel ordered him to stop and build a church to house the remains of the holy man.

Another legend relates how the spirit of St. Andrew appeared to a Pictish king called Hungus on the eve of a crucial battle against Saxon invaders, urging him to join forces with the Scots. As a further token of his support, a cloud formation resembling a saltire cross materialized in the sky during the course of the battle, and this spurred on the united army to defeat the English.

Angus, Aonghas

This is an ancient celtic name, meaning 'unique choice' and pronounced *AYNG-us*. It has important, historical overtones in Scotland, since Oenghus was one of the three sons of Erc, who helped to found the kingdom of Dalriada in Argyll. The name can also be linked with Hungus, a famous king of the Picts. Angus has retained its popularity into modern times and the Gaelic form, Aonghas, is also well used. Its profile has been raised by two distinguished poets, Aonghas Caimbeul (1903–82) and Aonghas MacNeacail (b.1942).

Archibald, meaning 'true' and 'bold'

ARCHIBALD, ARCHIE

THIS EVOLVED FROM AN OLD GERMAN NAME *Ercanbald*, from the elements *ercan* ('true') and *bald* ('bold') – in religious terms it was used to signify strength and solidity. It was introduced into Britain by the Normans, but always proved more popular in Scotland than in England. In particular, it was a favorite with the Douglas and Campbell clans. Archibald Douglas (1449–1513) gained the colorful nickname of Archibald 'Bell the Cat', after daring to confront the henchmen of James III. More recently, the novelist A.J. Cronin's (1896–1981) use of initials concealed the fact that his first name was Archibald.

B

BEATHAN, BEAN

THIS COMES FROM *beatha*, a Gaelic word for 'life' and is pronounced *bu-han*. It was a popular name in the Middle Ages, largely because of the cult of St. Bean, the 11th-century Bishop of Mortlach. Further proof of its popularity can be found in the surname Macbeth ('son of Beathan' or 'son of life'). In later years, it was increasingly anglicized as Benjamin.

Robert the Bruce (ruled 1306–29)

BRUCE

THE BRUCES WERE A NORMAN FAMILY, who probably took their name from the castle of Brix, near Cherbourg. They migrated to Scotland during the reign of David I (1124–53) and came to prominence through the exploits of Robert the Bruce (ruled 1306–29). Subsequently, generations of children have drawn inspiration from the tale of this famous Scottish hero, stiffening his resolve after watching the tireless efforts of a humble spider. Even so, the use of Bruce as a forename can only be traced back to the 18th century. Since then, the name has crossed many national boundaries and Bruce has now become a byword for an Australian.

St Columba
(c. 521-97)

C

CALLUM, CALUM

THIS COMES FROM the Latin word *columba*, which means 'dove'. It
owes its popularity to the crucial role played by St. Columba
(c.521–97), during Scotland's conversion to Christianity. Born in
Ireland, he migrated to Scotland in 563, founding an important
monastery on the island of Iona. From there, he launched a number of
missions into Pictish territory. One of these is said to have resulted in
the conversion of Brude, the King of the Picts.

*Cameron, meaning
'crooked nose'*

CAMERON

IN THE HIGHLANDS, Cameron originated as a nickname for someone
with a 'crooked nose' (*cam-shrón* in Gaelic). By contrast, the Lowland
branches of the clan are thought to have a territorial origin, from the
lands of Cameron near Edinburgh. In recent years, its use as a
forename has become widespread and, in 1999, it was the 4th most
popular boy's name in Scotland. In the US, it is now sometimes used
as a girl's name.

CLYDE

THIS NAME ORIGINATED IN SCOTLAND, but is now used more
extensively in the US and Caribbean. It comes from the River Clyde,
which flows through Glasgow and south-western Scotland. The source
of this word is uncertain, though some believe that it was named after a
British goddess called Clud or Clòta. In recent times, the name has
been associated with the gospel singer, Clyde McPhatter (1933–72),
and the bank robber Clyde Barrow, whose crimes formed the basis of
the Oscar-winning film, *Bonnie and Clyde* (1967).

Colin, the anglicized
form of Cailean

COLIN

IN ENGLAND and in some parts of Europe, this name developed as a
pet form of Nicholas. In Scotland, however, it stemmed from a
completely different source. There, it was the anglicized form of
Cailean, which means a 'cub' or 'young one'. The name became
particularly popular with the Campbells and the Mackenzies. The chief
of the Campbell clan is always called *MacCailean Mor*, in honor of Sir
Colin Campbell, the ancestor of the dynasty.

COLL

THIS TRADITIONAL CELTIC NAME comes from the Gaelic word *colla*, which means 'chief'. In Scottish mythology, Colla Uais is cited as an ancient Irish prince, who ruled over northern Britain, before the arrival of Scottish settlers. The MacDonalds claimed him as an ancestor, describing themselves as the Clan Cholla ('children of Coll'). In the Middle Ages, the name was often used as a diminutive for Nicholas.

COMPTON

THIS UNCOMMON NAME owes its occasional usage to the remarkable success of Sir Compton Mackenzie (1883–1972). Compton was actually his surname, but he added 'Mackenzie' to emphasize his Scottish roots. A prolific novelist, he settled on the island of Barra in 1928, where he wrote some of his best-loved comedies of Scottish manners. These include *The Monarch of the Glen* (1941), *Whisky Galore* (1947) and *Rockets Galore* (1957).

CONSTANTINE

THIS ORIGINATED AS A LATIN NAME, taken from a word for 'steadfast' (*constans*). In the West, it is chiefly associated with the Roman emperor, Constantine the Great (c.285–337), though his reputation as a champion of Christianity made the name popular in many countries. There were three Scottish monarchs called Constantine, as well as a king of the Picts (Constantine MacFergus, 789–820). The name is now uncommon in Scotland, although the female form (Constance) is still in use.

Cormac, 'raven son'

CORMAC

THE ORIGINS OF THIS ancient Celtic name are uncertain. Popular interpretations of its meaning include 'raven son' (_cor_ + _mac_) and 'chariot lad' (_corb_ + _mac_). The name was mentioned in the writings of St. Adamnan (d.704), an early abbot of Iona, but in recent times it has mainly been used as a surname in Scotland. The MacCormacks can be traced back to the 12th century, when Gillecrist mac Cormaic was cited in a charter pertaining to the Abbey of Deer.

CRAIG

THIS IS AN OLD CELTIC NAME stemming from _carraig_, which means a 'rock' or 'crag'. In common with many other names which derive from geographical features, it was originally used as a surname. In recent years, it has been associated with Craig Brown, the manager of Scotland's soccer team, and Craig McLachlan, a television star and singer.

Cuthbert

Cuthbert is an anglo-saxon name, deriving from *cuth* ('famous') and *beorht* ('bright'). It gained wide currency north of the border, however, through the popularity of St. Cuthbert (d.687). He is chiefly associated with Lindisfarne in Northumbria, but his ministry also took him to Galloway and the Borders. Kirkcudbright ('the Church of Cuthbert') is one of several Scottish sites, which bear his name. Many legends are told of him. While staying at one remote Scottish monastery, he would wade out into the freezing sea, right up to his armpits, and chant the praises of the Lord. Then, on returning to the shore, two otters would follow him and warm him up, by licking his feet and rubbing their coats against his skin. As a name, Cuthbert fell out of favor at the time of the First World War, when it was used as a slang term for a man who evaded military service.

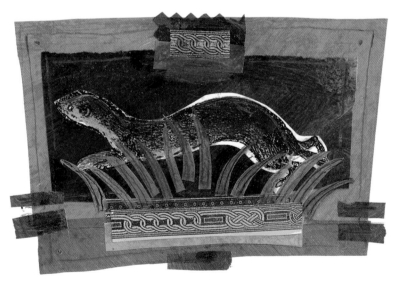

St Cuthbert (d.687)

D

DAVID

A HEBREW NAME MEANING 'beloved', this has been popular in Scotland since the Middle Ages. David I (ruled 1124–53) was an influential monarch, responsible for bringing to the north many of the Norman families (Balliol, Bruce, Stewart) who would shape the nation's future. The name has also figured largely in Scottish literature – David Balfour was the hero of Stevenson's *Kidnapped* (1886).

DONALD

THIS STEMS FROM DOMHNALL ('mighty ruler'), one of the oldest Celtic names. It was imported from Ireland and was used by a number of early Scottish kings. Domhnall Breac became King of the Scots in 629, while Domhnall MacAlpin ruled from 859 to 863. In the 13th century, Donald of Islay founded the MacDonald clan and, subsequently, Donald of Reay gained notoriety as a Wizard Laird. Legend has it that the devil stole his shadow, while he was teaching him the dark arts.

DONOVAN

Donovan STEMS FROM the Gaelic words *donn* ('brown' or 'kingly') and *dubh* ('black'), together with the diminutive *-an*. This suggests that it was originally a nickname, meaning something along the lines of 'little dark king' or 'little dark one'. Surviving principally as a surname, it gained a new lease of life in the 1960s through the popularity of the Scottish folksinger, Donovan (Donovan Leitch, b.1946).

DOUGLAS

This is BOTH THE NAME of a famous clan and a hugely popular forename. It means 'black stream' (from the Gaelic words *dubh* and *glas*), and was originally used as a nickname for a number of Scottish rivers. The forename is current throughout the English-speaking world. In recent times, it has been associated with the swashbuckling actors, Douglas Fairbanks Snr. and Jnr., and with the military supremo, General Douglas MacArthur (1880–1964).

Douglas, meaning 'black stream'

DREW

THIS IS NORMALLY REGARDED AS an abbreviated form of Andrew
which, as the name of nation's patron saint, was extremely popular
in Scotland. However, it has also been linked with other forenames.
In particular, it is associated with the Germanic name Drogo, which
was introduced into Britain by the Normans, who rendered it as
Dru. Some have also suggested, rather less feasibly, that there is a
connection with the Celtic term *draoi* ('dealer in magic'). In the
United States, Drew is sometimes used as a girl's name, notably by
the actress Drew Barrymore.

DUGALD, DOUGAL

JUST AS FINGAL WAS the Scottish nickname for fair-haired Vikings,
so Dougal was term for dark-haired ones (from *dubh* – 'dark' and *gall*
– 'stranger'). It is said to have been applied specifically to Danes. Dubh,
the son of Malcolm I, was briefly King of the Scots (962–7), while
Dubhgall, the eldest son of Somerled, Lord of the Isles, was the
founder of the MacDougall clan.

DUNCAN

THIS IS THE ANGLICIZED FORM of Donnchadh, an ancient Celtic
name which means 'brown warrior'. In Scotland, it was borne by an
8th-century saint and two medieval kings. The first of these, Duncan I
(ruled 1034–40), has found lasting fame as the royal victim in
Shakespeare's *Macbeth* (c.1606). He was a genuine historical figure,
although the details of his stabbing were invented by the dramatist. In
fact, he was slain in battle.

Duncan 1
(ruled 1034-40)

E

Eachann

THIS TRADITIONAL CELTIC NAME, pronounced *YAH-han*, is made up
from the Gaelic words, *each* ('horse') and *donn*. The latter can mean
both 'brown' and 'king', which has created a certain amount of
ambiguity about the name, raising the possibility that it was originally
applied to a horse-deity. In medieval records, the name was spelled
'Achyne' or 'Echdoun', while Eachann Bacach (fl. 1650) was a poet in
the service of the Macleans of Duart. It is now frequently anglicized as
Hector, although there is no real connection between the two names.

Eoghan

THERE ARE SEVERAL POSSIBLE EXPLANATIONS for the origin of this
name (pronounced *YO-en*). The most widely-held view is that it stems
from *Eugenios*, which means 'well-born'. As such, it is traditionally
anglicized as Eugene. It has also been suggested that it comes from a
Celtic word for 'son of the yew' (a legacy of ancient tree worship). The
name is principally associated with Ireland, featuring prominently in its
legends, but it was also well used in Scotland. Eoghan MacLachlainn
(1775–1822), for example, was a noted poet and translator.

ERIC

ERIC IS A SCANDINAVIAN NAME meaning 'ever brave', which was introduced into Scotland by Viking settlers. Erik Slagbrellis, for example, was an early ruler of Caithness and Orkney. The name underwent a revival in the 19th century, perhaps as a result of the popular children's book, *Eric: or Little by Little* (1858). Since then, it has also been associated with Eric Liddell (1902–45), the athlete whose story was featured in *Chariots of Fire*, the novelist Eric Linklater (1899–1974) and Eric Blair (the real name of the writer, George Orwell, 1903–50).

ERSKINE

ALTHOUGH CHIEFLY FAMILIAR as a surname, this is also used as a first name. Its origins are territorial, deriving from the Barony of Erskine in Renfrewshire. The Erskines were a powerful family, who came to hold the earldom of Mar. As a forename, it is most closely associated with Erskine Childers (1870–1922), the political writer and novelist. He is best remembered for his thriller, *The Riddle of the Sands* (1903), which was turned into a film in 1978.

EWAN, EUAN

LIKE EUGENE, this is frequently regarded as an anglicized form of Eoghan. It probably comes from the Gaelic word *eobhann* ('youth'). It flourished initially as the surname of the MacEwens, who were descended from a 13th-century figure called Ewen of Otter. More recently, it has become popular as a forename. Ewan MacColl (1915–89) was an influential Scottish folksinger, while the actor Ewan McGregor found fame in *Trainspotting* and *Star Wars: The Phantom Menace*.

EWART

THE EWARTS (PRONOUNCED *YOU-WART*) were an old Galloway family, who took their name from a place in Northumberland. This in turn derived from the Old English *ea-weorth* ('river enclosure'). The forename may stem from this or from a Norman variant of Edward. Either way, the popularity of the forename appears to have followed its use by the British Prime Minister, William Ewart Gladstone (1809–98). More recently, it has been associated with Ewart Mackintosh (1893–1917), the poet who was killed on the Western Front.

F

FERGUS, FERGIE

FERGUS IS A POPULAR GAELIC NAME, deriving from *fear* ('man')
and *gus* ('vigor'). According to tradition, Fergus, the son of Erc,
founded the Scottish kingdom of Dalriada. Also known as Fergus the
Great, legend also relates that he was responsible for transporting the
Irish coronation stone (the Lia Fáil) to Scotland, but refused to
return it. In time, this became known as the Stone of Scone (or
'Stone of Destiny'). The latter was always treated with great
reverence, because it was believed to be 'Jacob's Pillow' – the stone he
slept upon when he dreamed of angels ascending a ladder to heaven
(Genesis XXVIII, 11-12).

FIFE, FYFE

AS A FORENAME, this is occasionally used for natives of the
'kingdom' of Fife. According to tradition, it owes its origins to Fib, one
of the seven sons of King Cruithne, the legendary ancestor of the
Picts. In recent times, its most famous bearer was the broadcaster and
journalist, Fyfe Robertson.

Fingal, the son of a giant

FINGAL

ORIGINALLY A NICKNAME applied to Viking invaders, this means 'fair stranger' (from *fionn* – 'fair' and *gall* – 'stranger'). The name gained fresh impetus in the 18th century, when James Macpherson made Fingal the central character in his Ossianic poems. Loosely based on the mythical Irish hero, Fionn mac Cumhaill, Fingal was the son of a giant and a fearless defender of the oppressed. One of his most notable, legendary exploits was to build a fairy bridge, linking the Giant's Causeway in Ireland with Fingal's Cave in Staffa.

FINLAY, FINDLAY

THIS IS THE ANGLICIZED FORM of an old Celtic name *Fionnlagh*, which means 'fair hero'. In early Scottish history, the name is chiefly associated with the father of Macbeth. He is variously documented as Findlaech or Finnleikr, the Mormaer of Moray. In later years, it was mainly used as a surname – as in the long-running UK television series, *Dr. Findlay's Casebook* – although examples of the forename can still be found. Finlay Currie (1878–1968) was one of Scotland's most versatile actors.

FORBES

INITIALLY USED EXCLUSIVELY as a surname, this derives from *forba-ais* ('at the land or place'). Until fairly recently, both the forename and the surname were pronounced as two syllables. The original Forbes estates were in Aberdeenshire. According to legend, they were granted to Ochonobar – the founder of the clan – after he killed a savage bear, which had been terrorising the district. In later years, the family became notorious for its long-running feud with the Gordons. This resulted in a number of violent encounters, the bloodiest of which was described in a celebrated ballad, *Edom o' Gordon*. Corgarff Castle in Aberdeenshire is said to be haunted by the ghostly screams of members of the Forbes family, who were butchered by their enemies.

Ochonobar, killer of a savage bear

Fraser, Frasier

THIS FAMOUS CLAN NAME comes from a Norman source. Its earliest form was de Frisselle or de Fresel. Eventually, this changed to Fraser, probably after a branch of the family added a strawberry plant (*fraisier*) to their armorial crest. The first recorded bearer of the name, Sir Simon Frasee, held lands in East Lothian, while in c.1160 Symon ffraser made a sizeable donation to the Abbey of Kelso. The use of Fraser as a first name only dates back to the early 20th century. In recent years, it has received a huge boost from the international success of the television comedy, *Frasier*. In the UK, the name was also popularized by the soap star, Frazer Hines.

Sir Simon Frasee

Gavin, 'May hawk'

G

GAVIN

THIS IS AN ANCIENT CELTIC NAME, which appears to come from *gwalchmai* ('white hawk' or 'May hawk'). In Arthurian legend, it was linked with Gawain, who was described in some sources as a Prince of Orkney. Subsequently, the name has been associated with Gavin Hamilton (1723–98), an illustrious painter; Gavin Maxwell (1914–69), the author of *Ring of Bright Water* (1960) and Gavin Hastings, the record-breaking rugby star.

GILCHRIST

IN THE MIDDLE AGES, *gille* ('servant') was attached as a prefix to a number of different names. These usually had religious overtones, suggesting a devotee or follower. Thus, Gilchrist was a 'servant of Christ', while Gillespie meant a 'servant of the bishop' and Gilmour 'a servant of (the Virgin) Mary'. Most of these later became surnames, but Gilchrist has survived as an occasional forename. In particular, it is remembered as the name of the sculptor, who created St. Martin's Cross on Iona.

Gille Iosa,
'servant of Jesus'

GILLIES

GILLIES (PRONOUNCED *GUIL-EES*) is the anglicized form of the
Gaelic words *Gille Iosa* ('servant of Jesus'), a name that was popular
in clerical circles. In c.1128, Gillise witnessed a royal charter at the
Abbey of Holyrood, while in 1264 Gylis, the son of Angus the
shoemaker, did homage to the Prior of St. Andrews. During the
18th century, the name evolved into Elias, but since then Gillies
has once again become the preferred version.

GLEN

THIS TOPOGRAPHICAL NAME comes from a Gaelic word, *gleann*
('valley'), which has entered the English language. In Scotland, it is
principally used as a surname, often relating to the owners of the Glen
estates in Peeblesshire. Its use as a forename is much more common in
the United States and Canada, where notable bearers have included the
actor, Glenn Ford, and the singer, Glen Campbell. It is sometimes also
employed as a female name, as with the actress Glenn Close.

GORDON

ORIGINALLY A FAMOUS CLAN NAME, this has now become firmly established as a popular forename. Its origins are thought to be territorial, stemming from *gordun* ('hill-fort'). The power of the chiefs of the Gordon clan was emphasized by their nickname – 'the Cock o' the North'. Gordon's popularity as a first name can be linked with both the mood of British patriotic fervor inspired by the bravery of General Gordon at the Siege of Khartoum (1884–5) and the popularity of George Gordon, better known as the poet Lord Byron.

'The Cock o' the North'

GRAHAM, GRAEME

ALTHOUGH THIS IS USUALLY REGARDED as a typically Scottish name, it actually derives from Grantham in Lincolnshire. As such, its literal meaning comes from the Old English words *grand* ('gravel') and *ham* ('homestead'). The alternative spelling stems from a family legend that a Caledonian warrior named Gram or Gramus led a raiding party against the Romans, breaching a section of the Antonine Wall. As a result, this area became known as 'Graeme's Dyke'.

GRANT

THIS COMES FROM THE FRENCH WORD *grand* ('great' or 'tall'), which was introduced by the Normans. As a family name, it seems to have emerged in Scotland, where it is associated with an ancient clan from Inverness. Its transition to a forename occurred in the United States, as a tribute to the 18th President, Ulysses S. Grant (1822–85).

GREGOR, GREGORY

STEMMING FROM A GREEK WORD *gregorios* ('watchful'), this name became popular with Christians, because of the associations with a shepherd watching over his flock. In Scotland, the oldest links are with Griogar, a legendary king, and Gregor of the Golden Bridles, the founder of the powerful MacGregor clan. In recent years, the name has been popularized by the successful Scottish film, *Gregory's Girl* (1980) and by the actor Gregor Fisher.

Gregor, the
watchful shepherd

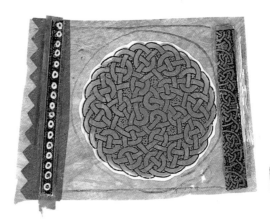

H

Hamish

This is a scottish variant of james, the equivalent of Seamus in Ireland. Sir Walter Scott featured a character called Hamish MacTavish in *The Highland Widow* (1827) and the name appears frequently in the novels of William Black (1841–98). More recently, Hamish Henderson (b.1919) has won acclaim for his verse and for his work in preserving the oral culture of Scottish tinkers. The name is often used as a byword for a Highlander.

Harry, Henry

This is a germanic name, which comes from *haim* ('home') and *ric* ('ruler'). It was introduced into Britain by the Normans. Henry was more popular in England than Scotland, although both David I and James VI had sons bearing this name. Conversely, the pet form Harry found greater favor north of the border. The minstrel known as Blind Harry (c.1440–c.1492) wrote an epic poem in praise of William Wallace, while Hugh MacLennan (1870–1950) chose the stage name 'Harry Lauder', when he was performing his music-hall act as a comical Scotsman.

HECTOR

Hector, 'horse-lord'

Hᴇᴄᴛᴏʀ ᴄᴏᴍᴇs ꜰʀᴏᴍ ᴀ ɢʀᴇᴇᴋ ᴡᴏʀᴅ, meaning 'to restrain' or 'hold fast'. The name is chiefly associated with the Trojan hero, who featured prominently in classical legend, but it also became popular in the Highlands during the Middle Ages. There, it was used to anglicize the Gaelic name, Eachann (literally 'a horse-lord'). Hector Boece (c.1465–1536) was one of Scotland's earliest historians and the ultimate source of much of the material in Shakespeare's *Macbeth*. Hector Macneill (1746–1818) was a poet and novelist, while Hector MacMillan (b.1929) is a dramatist.

HUGH, SHUG

Tʜɪs ɪs ᴀ ɢᴇʀᴍᴀɴɪᴄ ɴᴀᴍᴇ meaning 'mind' or 'spirit', which was brought to Britain by the Normans. It rapidly became popular in Scotland, where it served as the anglicized form of three separate Gaelic names – Aodh, Eoghan and Uisdean. Aodh means 'fire', while Uisdean was a borrowing from an Old Norse name, *Eystein* ('ever stone'). Hughie, Shug and Shuggie are all recognized pet forms.

Hunter

Principally used as a surname, this has been associated with a number of historic, Scottish families. The most notable of these were the official huntsmen of the Dukes of Normandy, who migrated to Scotland during the reign of David I (1124–53). They were granted the lands of Hunter's Toune (now Hunterston) in Ayrshire. As a forename, this is most closely associated with Hunter S. Thompson, the controversial author of *Fear and Loathing in Las Vegas* (1972).

Hunter, a historic
family name

I

IAIN, IAN, EOIN

THESE ARE GAELIC FORMS OF JOHN, which means 'God is gracious'.
Iain and Ian are pronounced *EE-an*, while Eoin is pronounced *YO-en*. The
name gave rise to several distinguished families, notably the MacKeans,
the MacKains, and the MacIans. None, however, were more tragic than
the MacIains for, as a sept of the MacDonalds, they were among the
clansmen butchered by Campbells at the Massacre of Glencoe (1692). In
recent years, the name has been well represented in the arts. Ian Hamilton
Finlay (b.1925) is one of Scotland's leading artists, while Iain Banks, Ian
McEwan and Iain Sinclair are fine, contemporary novelists.

IVAR

A LEGACY OF SCOTLAND'S VIKING PAST, this is an Old Norse name,
made up of elements meaning 'yew' and 'warrior'. Ivar the Boneless
raided the prehistoric tomb of Maes Howe (Orkneys), carrying off 'a
great treasure that was hidden there'. The MacIver family became a
sept of the Campbell clan. Their own name was outlawed in 1688,
when Iver of Asknish took part in a rebellion.

James
Macpherson
(d. 1700)

J

JAMES

A BIBLICAL NAME MEANING 'supplanter', this evolved from the Latin forms *Jacobus* and *Jacomus*. The name gained great popularity in Western Europe, because of St. James's reputation as a pilgrim, symbolized by the scallop shell which was worn as a badge. In Scotland, there were seven Stuart kings called James (or eight, including the 'Old Pretender'), and the name is also linked with the inventor James Watt (1736–1819) and the writer James (J.M.) Barrie (1860–1937). In popular folklore, James Macpherson was the Scottish equivalent of Robin Hood. While awaiting execution, he composed a famous fiddle tune, *Macpherson's Rant*, which he played beneath the gallows.

Jock, a Highland soldier

JOCK

THIS IS A PET FORM OF JOHN, the equivalent of Jack in England. Within Scotland, it is used as a nickname for a Highland soldier; elsewhere, it is a byword for any Scotsman. 'Jock Tamson's Bairns' is a Scottish idiom for the human race. *Stop yer tickling, Jock* (1904) was one of the best-known songs of Sir Harry Lauder (1870–1950).

JOHN

THIS IS A HEBREW NAME, meaning 'God is gracious'. Initially, its use was mainly confined to the Byzantine empire, but it became popular in the West at the time of the Crusades. The Gaelic form, Iain, has a more authentic Caledonian flavor, but John is also widely used. John Balliol (ruled 1292–6) was briefly and ignominiously King of the Scots. The northernmost tip of Scotland, John o' Groat's, was supposedly named after a 15th-century Dutchman, John de Groot, who ran the Orkney ferry. According to legend, his eight sons were so quarrelsome that he built an octagonal house and an octagonal dining-table, so that none of them could claim precedence or favoritism.

K

Keir

ORIGINALLY THIS WAS A SURNAME, deriving from the Old Norse word *kjarr* ('brushwood') or from the Gaelic *caer* ('a fortress'). Its use as a forename was undoubtedly due to the popularity of James Keir Hardie (1856–1915), one of the founders of the Scottish Labour party. Keir was actually his mother's maiden name.

James Keir Hardie
(1856–1915)

Keith

ORIGINALLY A PLACE-NAME, this has now become one of the most popular Scottish Christian names. It comes from the Gaelic word *ceiteach*, which signifies a 'wood' or 'forest'. There may also be links with the Welsh word *coedwig*, which has a similar meaning. Medieval records specify that a succession of Norman lords held the lands of Keth in East Lothian from the 11th century. Later, the family held the hereditary post of Earl Marischal.

KELVIN

THIS IS A MODERN NAME, which has only been in use since the 1920s. In common with Clyde, it was inspired by a river which runs through the city of Glasgow. The Belfast-born physicist William Thomson (1824–1907), who was a professor at Glasgow University, took the title of Baron Kelvin of Largs (1892). The Kelvin temperature scale is named after him.

Kenneth
MacAlpin
(d.858)

KENNETH

IT APPEARS THAT KENNETH is an amalgam of two separate Gaelic names, *Cinaed* ('born of fire') and *Coinneach* ('handsome'). The name has long been popular in Scotland, because of the achievements of Kenneth MacAlpin. In 843, he managed to unite the Picts and the Scots under a single crown, forming the nucleus of a genuine nation. As a result, he is traditionally regarded as the first King of Scotland.

KYLE

THIS NAME HAS GEOGRAPHICAL ORIGINS. A kyle is a Scottish term for a narrow strait (from the Gaelic word *caol*), as in the Kyle of Lochalsh. Used as a forename in the United States, the actors Kyle MacLachlan, who starred in the cult television show *Twin Peaks*, and Kyle Eastwood, the son of Clint Eastwood, are examples.

L

Lachlan, Lachlann

This ancient name (pronounced *LAK-lan*) is a reminder of Scotland's Scandinavian heritage. It means 'lakeland' and was used to describe the Viking raiders, who traveled across from their native fjords. The name was sufficiently popular to give rise to a MacLachlan clan and a Castle Lachlan. It is frequently shortened to Lachie or Lacky, and there is a female form, Lachina.

Lachlan, meaning 'Lakeland'

Lennox

This originated as a surname, which probably derives from the district of Levenach, meaning a 'smooth stream'. Alternatively it may stem from *leamhán*, a Gaelic word for an 'elm grove'. As a clan name, Lennox has a long pedigree, but only in the 20th century has it come to be used as a forename. Sir Lennox Berkeley (1903–89) was a noted composer, while the meteoric success of Lennox Lewis, the world heavyweight boxing champion, has given the name added charisma.

Leslie

Initially used purely as a surname, this is now also a popular forename. Its origins are territorial, coming from the Barony of Lesslyn, which was granted to a brother of William the Lion in the late 12th century. This in turn may stem from *leas cuilinn*, which is Gaelic for 'garden of hollies'. Its use as a Christian name can only be dated back to 1832. In modern times, the most celebrated bearer of the name was the actor Leslie Howard (1890–1943), who starred in *Gone with the Wind* (1939).

Ludovic

This evolved from a Germanic name, Ludwig (from *hlud* – 'fame' and *wig* – 'warrior'), which was Latinized as Ludovicus. It became popular in the Highlands in the 17th century, because of the phonetic similarities to a Gaelic name meaning 'servant of the Lord'. In 1639, for example, Ludovic Lindsay inherited the title of 16th Earl of Crawford, while in the same period Sir Ludovick Gordon became Baronet of Gordonstoun.

M

MAGNUS

MAGNUS IS THE LATIN WORD FOR 'GREAT'. As a name, this became popular throughout Europe, following the exploits of Charlemagne (Carolus Magnus, 742–814). It was much used in Scandinavia and, from there, it spread to the Highlands and the Northern Isles. Magnus Barelegs was King of Norway (1093–1103) and ruled for a time over the Hebrides and Kintyre. St. Magnus (d.1116) was joint ruler in the Orkneys, where he was murdered by his cousin. The Islands' cathedral at Kirkwall is dedicated to him, and there is a legend that he appeared in a vision to Robert the Bruce on the eve of Bannockburn.

St. Magnus
(d.1116)

Malcolm

This name was designed to honor the memory of a famous Scottish saint, for it stems from the Gaelic *Maol Coluim* ('servant of Columba'). It was given to four medieval kings, the most notable of whom was Malcolm III (ruled 1058–93), also known as Malcolm Canmore ('big head' or 'great chief'). He came to the throne after defeating Macbeth at the Battle of Lumphanan (1057), and ending the brief reign of his stepson, Lulach the Simple. Malcolm's reign coincided with the Norman invasion in the south, and he used this opportunity to make repeated incursions into northern England. He was also the husband of St. Margaret. In the modern era, the name has been associated with Sir Malcolm Campbell (1885–1948), who set world speed records on both land and water.

Maxwell

This famous Scottish name comes from Maccus' *wael* ('a pool'), a salmon pool on the River Tweed which once belonged to a Saxon lord called Maccus. Its use as a forename is most closely associated with William Maxwell Aitken, Lord Beaverbrook (1879–1964), the Canadian-born press baron.

Melvin, Melvyn, Melville

Melville was the name of a Norman baronial family, who migrated to Scotland in the 12th century. It preserves the memory of their French estates at Malleville (literally 'bad town'). Melvin developed later, as a variant of Melville, but it has proved a much more popular choice as a forename.

Malcolm III (ruled 1058-93)

MUNGO

THIS IS A CELTIC NICKNAME meaning 'my pet'. It is most closely
associated with St. Mungo (d.612), the patron saint of Glasgow,
whose real name was Kentigern. He was a missionary in the
Strathclyde region and is believed to have founded the first church at
Glasgow. The city arms include a memento of one of his miracles, a
fish with a ring. A Scottish queen named Langueth gave her ring to a
lover. Unfortunately for her, the king recognized it on the man's
hand, stole it while he was sleeping and hurled it into the river. Then
he called the queen to him and demanded to see the trinket. She was
in despair until Mungo came to her aid. In a vision, he saw that the
ring had been swallowed by a salmon, which had just been caught by
one of his monks. Swiftly, the jewel was retrieved and the queen's
honor was saved.

St Mungo (d.612)

Murdo of the Deer

MURDOCH, MURDO

AN ANGLICIZED VERSION of the Celtic name Murchadh or
Muireadhach, which comes from a word for 'the sea' (*muir*). In Scottish
folklore, Murdo of the Deer was an ageing huntsman. As he took aim
at a stag on one occasion, the creature turned into a fairy, who mocked
his silver hair. A fervent Christian, Murdo declared that God could
make him young again – which He duly did. In historical terms,
Murdoch Nisbet (fl. 1520) wrote a Scots version of the New
Testament, while Murdoch, Duke of Albany, held the post of Regent
during James I's reign.

MURRAY, MORAY

ORIGINALLY, this was the name of a powerful Scottish family,
so-called because they owned the lands of Moray. Its use as a
forename may well have been prompted by the similarity to the Irish
name, Muiredach or Muireadhach (meaning 'man of the sea').

N

NEIL

THIS IS AN ANGLICIZED VERSION of the popular Irish name,
Niall. Its derivation is disputed, but it probably came from *nía*
('champion'). Viking settlers adopted the name, rendering it as
Njal, while in England it was Latinized as Nigellus (later Nigel).
The Irish origins of the name remained to the fore. The MacNeils
claimed descent from Irish ancestors, while many Scots chose to
spell the name 'Niel'. The best-known example of this is Niel
Gow (1727–1807), the celebrated fiddler. In his day, he was so
famous that Burns made a special detour to meet him during his
tour of the Highlands.

NICOL

THIS IS A DIMINUTIVE OF Nicholas, a popular forename which was
introduced into Britain by the Normans. Its origins lie in the Greek
words *nike* ('victory') and *laos* ('people'). The name has long been
popular in Scotland, giving rise to both the MacNicol and Nicolson
families. Nicol Jarvie was a key character in Scott's *Rob Roy* (1817),
while Nicol Williamson is a distinguished actor of stage and screen.

O

OSSIAN

ALTHOUGH RARELY USED TODAY, this name, pronounced *USH-en*, was once famous throughout Europe. Ossian was the narrator in an epic cycle of poems, published by James Macpherson (1736–96). He claimed that the verses were the fragmentary remains of an ancient store of oral Gaelic literature, though this was hotly disputed by some experts. Ossian himself was loosely based on a mythical Irish hero called Oisín, the son of the Celtic warrior, Fionn mac Cumhaill. His name means 'little deer', a reference to the legend that his mother was transformed into a fawn by an evil druid, and the young Oisín was reared in the wild until he was seven years old .

Oisín, son of Fionn mac Cumhaill

R

Ramsay, Ramsey

Principally used as a surname, this is thought to have its origins in an English place-name, Ramsey in Huntingdonshire. This in turn stems from the Old English words, *hramsa* ('wild garlic') and *eg* ('island'). Scotland had strong links with the county in the 12th century: David I's wife was Matilda of Huntingdon and he took many local retainers with him, when he travelled north in 1124 to claim his throne. As a forename, this is principally associated with Ramsay MacDonald (1866–1937), the British Prime Minister, who was born in Lossiemouth.

Ramsay
MacDonald
(1866–1937)

RANALD, RONALD

THIS IS AN ANGLICIZED VERSION of a Celtic name, Raghnall, which in turn stems from the Old Norse Rognvald. The latter, which is composed of *regin* ('advice') and *valdr* ('ruler'), was used extensively during Scotland's Viking period. Rognvald Brusason and Rognvald Eysteinsson ruled over the Orkneys, while Rognvald Godrodarson was a king of the Hebrides. During the Middle Ages, the name was often anglicized as Ronald, Reginald, or Reynold, but Ranald remains a popular name in its own right.

Rannulfr, meaning 'shield-wolf'

RANDAL

ORIGINALLY AN OLD NORSE NAME, this derives from Rannulfr, which means 'shield-wolf'. As such, it was a popular variant of Randolph. In Scotland, the name is closely associated with *Lord Randal*, one of the most familiar songs listed in Child's *English and Scottish Ballads* (1882). Bob Dylan used the tune as the basis for *A Hard Rain's a Gonna Fall*.

RANULF, RANULPH

THIS EVOLVED FROM AN OLD SCANDINAVIAN NAME Reginulfr, which is made up of *regin* ('advice') and *œlfr* ('wolf'). It was brought to Scotland by Viking raiders. The name is occasionally linked with Randolph, although this actually stems from Rannulfr ('shield' plus 'wolf'). In recent years, the name has been popularized by the Polar explorer, Ranulph Fiennes.

Ranulph

ROBERT, RAB, RABBIE

THIS IS ACTUALLY A GERMANIC NAME, made up of the elements *hrod* ('fame') and *berht* ('bright'). It has always been popular north of the border, however, because of the associations with Scotland's most famous sons – Robert the Bruce (ruled 1306–29) and Robbie Burns (1759–96). In addition, Robert Adam (1728–92) is widely regarded as Scotland's greatest architect.

Rory

Rory is a phonetic rendering of the Gaelic name Ruaraidh, which means 'red king'. It is sometimes anglicized as Roderick, although this actually comes from a Germanic source. In c.1131 Ruadri, the Mormaer of Mar, was cited in the *Book of Deer*. He was also Latinized as *Rothri comes* ('Count Ruadri') in the foundation charter of Scone. In recent years, the name has been popularized by the actor Rory Calhoun, and the Scottish folk musician Rory Gallagher.

Ross

Originally a surname, this is now one of the most popular Scottish forenames. It comes from the Gaelic *ros*, meaning a 'cape' or 'headland'. The Earls of Ross can trace their line back to the 13th century, but examples of the forename only appear to date from the 1840s. In recent years, the name has been popularized by the US politician, Ross Perot.

Ross, meaning 'headland'

Roy

THIS IS AN ANCIENT CELTIC NAME, which comes from *ruadh* ('red') and was commonly applied as a nickname to people with red hair. Its use as a baptismal name increased dramatically, after the exploits of the outlaw Rob Roy MacGregor (1671–1734) were turned into a novel (1817) by Sir Walter Scott. Although he spent much of his life as a farmer, Rob Roy acquired the reputation of a latter-day Robin Hood, helping the oppressed while also attempting to further the Jacobite cause. The name received an added stimulus in the 1940s, when Roy Rogers starred as a singing cowboy in a number of Hollywood films.

The 'Ruthven Raid' (1582)

Ruthven

ALTHOUGH PRINCIPALLY KNOWN AS A SURNAME (pronounced *RIV-en*), this is also used occasionally as a forename. It derives from the Barony of Ruthven in Angus, which was adopted as a family name by Sweyn, son of Thor, in the 13th century. For a time, it had scandalous overtones, following the 'Ruthven Raid' of 1582, when James VI was kidnapped, and the name was actually banned in 1600 (repealed 1641). In recent times, its principal bearer has been Ruthven Todd (1914–78), the poet, teacher and publisher, who ran the *Weekend Press*.

S

Scott

THIS NAME HAS AN OBVIOUS patriotic appeal for people with Scottish ancestry. Initially, it was used in border areas or, within Scotland itself, as a reference to Gaelic-speakers. It has also proved very popular in expatriate Scottish communities. The original Scots were an Irish tribe, who migrated to Argyll in c.500 and founded the colony of Dalriada. In modern times, the name has been associated with the novelist, F. Scott Fitzgerald (1896–1940), and the singer, Scott Walker.

Sholto, meaning 'sower'

SHOLTO

THIS IS A RARE EXAMPLE of a name that has been employed almost exclusively by a single clan. At the start of the 18th century, genealogists declared that the Douglas family was descended from Sioltaich Dubh Glas ('fruitful black stream'). The literal meaning of *sioltach* is 'sower', but it also implies 'fruitfulness' or 'fertility'. Since the initial claim was made, Sholto has been used by many generations of Douglases.

SINCLAIR

THE SINCLAIR CLAN came from Norman baronial stock. They took their name from the manor of Saint-Clair-sur-Elle, which the family had previously owned. They came to Britain at the time of the Conquest (1066), when Walderne de Sancto Claro joined the train of William I. In the UK, Sinclair is still regarded principally as a surname, but its use as a forename is more popular in the United States, perhaps as a result of the success of the novelist, Sinclair Lewis (1885–1951). He is chiefly remembered for *Elmer Gantry* (1927), his tale of a sham minister, which was turned into an Oscar-winning film (1960).

SOMERLED, SORLEY

THIS NAME (PRONOUNCED *SUM-er-led*) evolved from a viking name
Sumarlithr, which means 'summer traveler' – a reference to the
Scandinavian practice of wintering at home and forming raiding
parties in the summer. The name was popular amongst Viking settlers,
particularly in the west. Somerled, a 12th-century Lord of Argyll, was
the ancestor of the Clan MacDonald. Both Somhairle, the Gaelic form
of the name, and Sorley, its anglicized counterpart, are still in current
use. In recent times, they have been closely associated with Somhairle
MacGill-Eain (Sorley MacLean), the Gaelic poet who has championed
the cause of his native language and culture.

STEWART, STUART

THESE NAMES HAVE A SPECIAL RESONANCE in Scottish history,
because of the royal house which occupied the throne for more than
300 years. In the 12th century, Walter Fitz Alan was appointed High
Steward of Scotland, an important hereditary post which involved the
management of the royal household and the collection of crown
revenues. The clan took its name from this job, changing the 'd' to a 't'
in the late 14th century. Stuart is the French spelling of the name,
which was adopted in the mid-16th century. The choice of Stewart as
a forename only dates back to the late 19th century, but it is now in
widespread use.

T

Tam

Tam is the scottish form of Thomas. It was popularized by Tam o' Shanter, the eponymous hero of one of Robbie Burns' most famous poems. Returrning home late from the inn one night, Tam saw a coven of witches dancing by Alloway kirk (church). He stopped to watch them, admiring in particular a pretty one in a *cutty sark* ('short shift'). The witches spotted him, however, and gave chase. Tam sped off, knowing he would be safe, if he could reach the river. His mare carried him there, though one of the witches tore out the beast's tail, just as she was crossing the bridge.

Tam o'shanter,
hero of Robbie Burns' famous poem

TORMOD, NORMAN

An ANCIENT CELTIC NAME pronounced *TOR-i-mod*, this stemmed from the Old Norse words for 'Thor' and 'mind'. It was frequently employed in the Hebrides, where Tormod, son of Leod, became the ancestor of the MacLeods of Skye. In time, the name became anglicized as Norman ('north man'), although Tormod is still in use. In recent years, it has become associated with the poet and children's writer Tormod Caimbeul (b.1942).

Thorketill

TORQUIL

This NAME, pronounced *TOR-kwil*, evolved from an ancient Scandinavian name, Thorketill, which is made up of 'Thor' and *ketill* ('a sacrificial cauldron'). It was imported into Scotland by the Vikings. There are several figures called Thorkel in the *Orkneyinga Saga*, which deals with the early history of the Orkneys. The Gaelic form of the name was Torcail, which in turn became anglicized as Torquil. In the 13th century, Leod had a son named Torquil, who became the ancestor of the MacLeods of Lewis.

W

WALLACE

THIS NAME IS A COMBINATION OF *welisc* (Old English) and *waleis* (Old French), both of which mean 'foreigner'. These terms were applied by invading Anglo-Saxons and Normans to the ancient Celtic peoples, whom they found in various parts of Britain, and they eventually formed the root of the word 'Welsh'. Wallace was used exclusively as a surname, until the time of Sir William Wallace (c.1270–1305). His victory over the English at Stirling Bridge (1297) and the barbarous nature of his subsequent execution made a lasting impact on the Scottish psyche. As a result, many parents chose this name for their children out of a sense of patriotism.

Sir William Wallace
(c.1270–1305)

Sir Walter Scott
(1771–1832)

WALTER

THE OLDEST FORM OF THIS NAME was Wealdhere, which was used in England before the Conquest. With the coming of the Normans, it was superseded by Waldhar, a Germanic name composed of *wald* ('rule') and *hari* ('army'). Walter has been in common use in Scotland since Norman times, but it received a huge boost in the early 19th century, through the writings of Sir Walter Scott (1771–1832). With such books as *The Lay of the Last Minstrel* (1805), *Rob Roy* (1817) and *Redgauntlet* (1824), he made the name famous throughout Europe.

WILLIAM

WILLIAM IS A GERMANIC NAME, composed of *wil* ('will') and *helm* ('helmet'). It was introduced into Britain by the Normans, arriving in Scotland with the first wave of invaders. William the Lion (ruled 1165–1214) was a robust Scottish monarch. His nickname is said to derive from the fact that he chose the lion rampant as Scotland's emblem. He also managed to confirm the country's independent status, following an agreement with Richard I of England (the so-called 'Quitclaim of Canterbury', 1189). William's patriotic achievements were echoed by his namesake, Sir William Wallace (c.1270–1305), who continued the struggle against the English. On a less exalted note, William was also the forename of both Burke and Hare, two of Scotland's most notorious criminals. They became known as the 'body-snatchers', after committing a series of murders in the 1820s, in order to provide corpses for anatomists.

There are several pet forms of William. The most common of these is Billy, as borne by the actor and comedian Billy Connolly. The most distinctively Scottish variant is Wullie. This is chiefly associated with *Oor Wullie*, a comic strip which has appeared in the *Scottish Sunday Post* since 1934, and which has become something of a national institution.

Kings & Queens of Scotland

The early history of the Scottish monarchy is complex and shadowy. From around 500 AD there were two separate royal lines: in the west, the Scots held the kingdom of Dalriada, while the Picts to the east had their own rulers. Kenneth MacAlpin was not the first man to hold both crowns – his real achievement was to make the union permanent. With further immigration from Scandinavia, this was the time that many of the most evocative Scottish names became prevalent.

Malcolm II was MacAlpin's last direct descendent. His successor, Duncan, was the son of Crinan the Thane, who held the abbacy of Dunkeld, the chief religious center in Scotland. This lent its name to the next royal dynasty, which survived until the late 13th century, when the premature death of the Maid of Norway prompted a succession crisis – with no fewer than 13 claimants to the throne.

Order was restored by the Stewarts, who ruled for over 300 years, until Queen Anne died without issue in 1702. Although the Old and Young Pretenders attempted to regain the throne, through the Jacobite rebellions of 1715 and 1745, the family's hold on power had ended.

Kenneth macAlpin
843–858

Donald I
858–863

Constantine I
863–877

Aed
877–878

Eochaid and Giric
878–889

Donald II
889–900

Constantine II
900–943

KENNETH MACALPIN

IN 843, KENNETH MACALPIN created Alba, the nucleus of the future Scottish nation, when he merged the domains of the Scots and the Picts. Kenneth was a Scot, but he may have had a Pictish mother. Later chronicles contain dark rumors that he invited the Pictish nobility to a banquet and then slaughtered them when they were drunk. He struggled to maintain his power against the Vikings, abandoning western bases and transferring the relics of St. Columba from Iona to a safer haven at Dunkeld.

MALCOLM I
943–954

INDULF
954–962

DUBH
962–967

CUILEAN
967–971

KENNETH II
971–995

CONSTANTINE III
995–997

KENNETH III
997–1005

MALCOLM II
1005–1034

HOUSE OF DUNKELD

DUNCAN I
1034–1040

MACBETH
1040–1057

LULACH (THE SIMPLE)
1057–1058

MALCOLM III (CANMORE)
1058–1093

MACBETH
1040–1057

UNLIKE THE TRAGIC KING in Shakespeare's play, the real Macbeth
was probably no more villainous than his contemporaries. He took the
crown by force after defeating and killing his cousin, Duncan I, at the
Battle of Pitgaveny (1040). After this, Macbeth ruled jointly with
Thorfinn of Orkney. His reign was comparatively peaceful and, in
1050, he went on a pilgrimage to Rome, where he 'scattered money
among the poor like seed'. He lost the throne in 1057, when
Malcolm III – Duncan's son – slew him at the Battle of Lumphanan.

DONALD III (DONALD BANE)
1093–1094

DUNCAN II
1094–1094

DONALD III AND EDMUND
1094–1097

EDGAR
1097–1107

ALEXANDER I
1107–1124

DAVID I
1124–1153

MALCOLM IV (THE MAIDEN)
1153–1165

WILLIAM THE LION
1165–1214

ALEXANDER II
1214–1249

ALEXANDER III
1249–1286

MARGARET (THE MAID OF NORWAY)
1286–1290

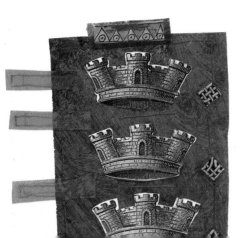

The Competitors

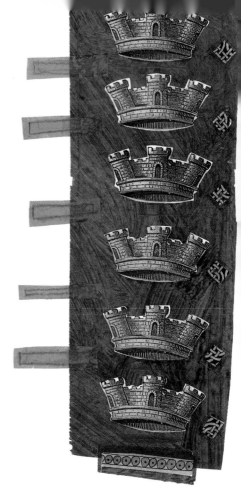

The First Interregnum
1290–1292

House of Balliol
John Balliol
1292–1296

The Second Interregnum
1296–1306

House of Bruce
Robert I (the Bruce)
1306–1329
David II
1329–1371

John Balliol
1292–1296

JOHN BALLIOL'S INEFFECTUAL RULE earned him the nickname
'Toom Tabard' ('Empty Coat'). He gained the throne only through the
support of Edward I, but for this favor the English king forced Balliol
to acknowledge him as his overlord. Further humiliations followed,
prompting the Scot to form an alliance with France and mount a
rebellion (1295) which Edward crushed after an overwhelming victory
at Dunbar (1296). Balliol was compelled to abdicate and, in a degrading
ceremony at Brechin, he was publicly stripped of his royal insignia.

JAMES I

FOLLOWING HIS CAPTURE IN 1406, James spent much of his youth at the English Court, where he became noted for his skill as a poet. His greatest work was *The Kingis Quair* ('The King's Book'), in which he described how a poet, imprisoned in a tower, fell in love with a maiden strolling in the grounds below. In fact, this was a true account of James's own romance with Lady Joan Beaufort, whom he married in 1423.

ROBERT II
1371–1390

ROBERT III
1390–1406

JAMES I
1406–1437

JAMES II
1437–1460

JAMES III
1460–1488

JAMES IV
1488–1513

JAMES V
1513–1542

HOUSE OF STUART

MARY, QUEEN OF SCOTS
1542–1567

JAMES VI
1567–1625

CHARLES I
1625–1649

THE COMMONWEALTH
1649–1660

CHARLES II
1660–1685

JAMES VII
1685–1688

WILLIAM AND MARY
1689–1702

ANNE
1702–1714

JACOBITE LINE

'JAMES VIII' (THE OLD PRETENDER)
('REIGNED' 1701–1766)

'CHARLES III' (BONNIE PRINCE CHARLIE)
('REIGNED' 1766–1788)

MARY, QUEEN OF SCOTS   1542–1567

THE DAUGHTER OF JAMES V, Mary gained the throne when she was just six days old. Deposed after her disastrous union with Lord Darnley, Mary fled to England in 1568, remaining a prisoner there until Elizabeth ordered her execution.